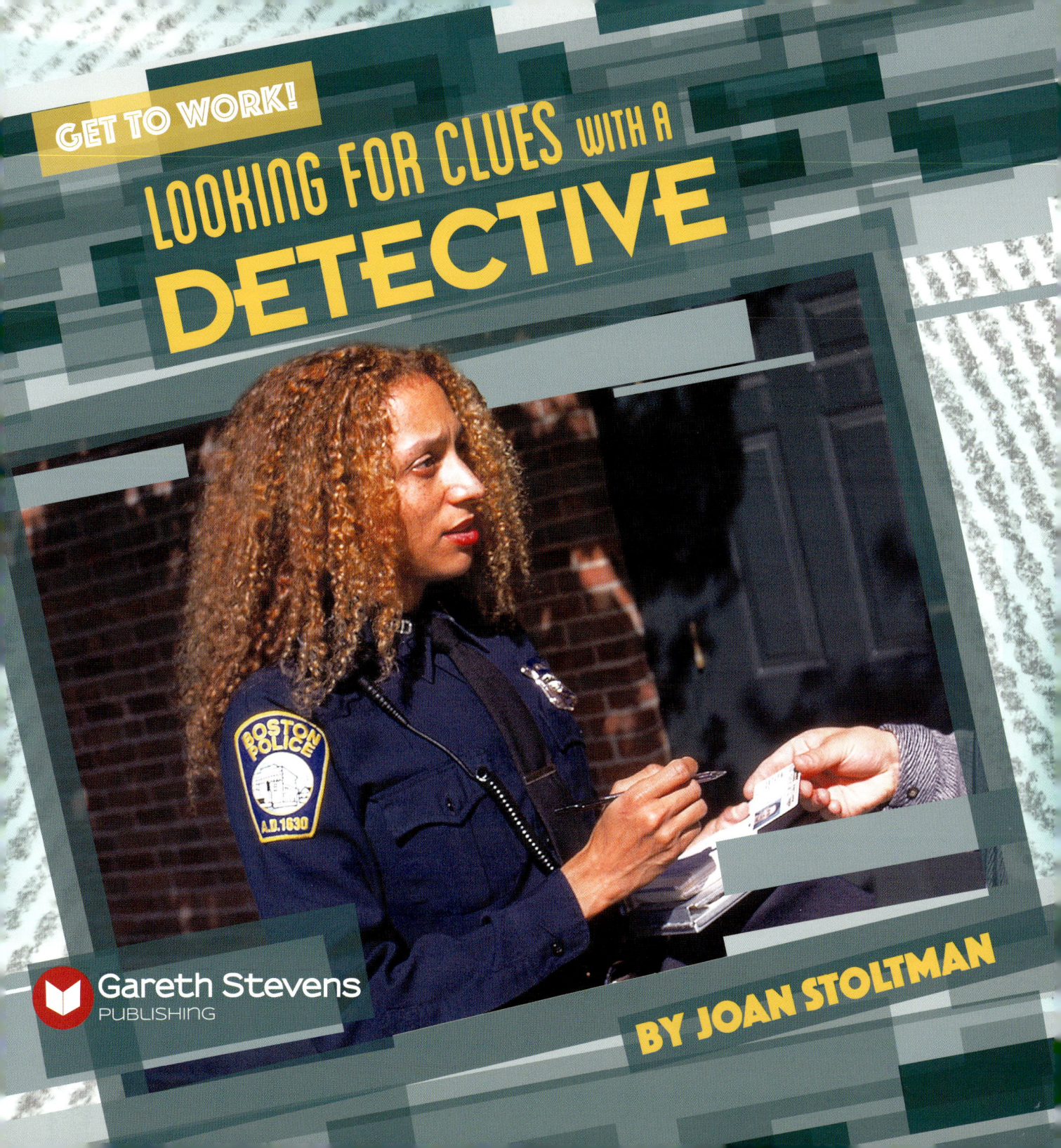

GET TO WORK!

LOOKING FOR CLUES WITH A
DETECTIVE

Gareth Stevens
PUBLISHING

BY JOAN STOLTMAN

Please visit our website, www.garethstevens.com. For a free color catalog of all our high-quality books, call toll free 1-800-542-2595 or fax 1-877-542-2596.

Cataloging-in-Publication Data

Names: Stoltman, Joan.
Title: Looking for clues with a detective / Joan Stoltman.
Description: New York : Gareth Stevens Publishing, 2019. | Series: Get to work! | Includes index.
Identifiers: ISBN 9781538212356 (pbk.) | ISBN 9781538212349 (library bound) | ISBN 9781538212332 (6 pack)
Subjects: LCSH: Criminal investigation–Juvenile literature. | Detectives–Juvenile literature. | Police–Equipment and supplies–Juvenile literature.
Classification: LCC HV8073.8 S7585 2018 | DDC 363.25028'4–dc23

Published in 2019 by
Gareth Stevens Publishing
111 East 14th Street, Suite 349
New York, NY 10003

Copyright © 2019 Gareth Stevens Publishing

Designer: Bethany Perl
Editor: Joan Stoltman

Photo credits: Cover, p. 1 Jeff Dunn/Photolibrary/Getty Images; pp. 1-24 (background) MaLija/Shutterstock.com; pp. 1-24 (rectangular banner) punsayaporn/Shutterstock.com; pp. 1-20, 22-24 (fingerprint background) Hans-Joachim Roy/Shutterstock.com; pp. 4-18 (text box) LoveVectorGirl/Shutterstock.com; p. 5 NEstudio/Shutterstock.com; p. 7 (police) Nuccio DiNuzzo/Chicago Tribune/Getty Images; p. 7 (files) Nirat.pix/Shutterstock.com; pp. 9 (detectives with evidence), 17 (detective conducting interview) Photographee.eu/Shutterstock.com; p. 10 Couperfield/Shutterstock.com; p. 11 A and N photography/Shutterstock.com; p. 13 (police school) Marsan/Shutterstock.com; p. 13 (graduation) a katz/Shutterstock.com; p. 15 Digital Vision/Photodisc/Getty Images; p. 19 mikeledray/Shutterstock.com; p. 21 (fingerprint background) domnitsky/Shutterstock.com; p. 21 (fingerprints) charobnica/Shutterstock.com; p. 21 (torn paper and tape) Flas100/Shutterstock.com.

Printed in the United States of America

CPSIA compliance information: Batch #CS18GS: For further information contact Gareth Stevens, New York, New York at 1-800-542-2595.

CONTENTS

Words in the glossary appear in **bold** type the first time they are used in the text.

WHAT'S A DETECTIVE?

A detective **solves** crimes and mysteries for a living. Cool, right? They do this by gathering clues after a crime. Sometimes the clues are right at the place where the crime happened, called a crime scene. These kinds of clues are called evidence, and they can help prove how the crime happened. Other clues are harder to find.

Detectives solve crimes to help people and to bring criminals to justice. It's a hard job with long hours and tricky mysteries, but somebody's got to do it!

STUDY A MYSTERY!

Have a librarian or parent help you pick a mystery book or movie. Write down notes for each character and clues. Can you solve the mystery before the end?

Detectives can also be called investigators or agents depending on where they work. They can work for state or national **law enforcement** groups, private companies—or even for themselves!

DETECTIVE, YOU'VE GOT A CASE

Clues can come from a number of **sources**, including the crime scene and people. Detectives interview witnesses and **victims** to get clues. They also question the people who are believed to have committed the crime, called suspects. They record many of these conversations, or talks, so that they can study them later.

After all the clues are followed, usually a detective is closer to knowing what happened. Then they put everything they've learned together with the evidence to solve the case—like a **puzzle**!

WATCH CLOSELY!

A person's **body language** sometimes shows what they're feeling, even if they don't say it! Detectives pay special attention to eyes and hands for clues when speaking with suspects, witnesses, and even victims. During your next conversation, take notes on what you hear the person say and what their face and hands are doing.

After every conversation, a detective must write notes and reports for the case file. This helps keep all the facts in order!

CASE FILES

THE MIND OF A DETECTIVE

The entire time a detective is speaking with anyone connected to a case, they're gathering evidence. They also use computers to find out more about the people and places that are connected to the case.

Detectives carefully consider every piece of **information** in the case. Sometimes clues leave them guessing, but usually they can find things to prove their guesses correct. When it's time to present a case to a judge, detectives can only talk about proof they know is true and complete.

Often, a few detectives work the same case! They check each other's work. They may even have different suspects!

9

LIFE AS A POLICE DETECTIVE

Many detectives work in police departments. Cases are given so that one detective doesn't get stuck with all the hard-to-solve cases. Police detectives work with police officers and forensic scientists on almost every case.

Big city detectives often specialize in certain kinds of crimes. Detectives can specialize in murders, robberies, illegal drugs, and other kinds of crimes. There are even detectives who **investigate** the police to make sure everyone is doing their job right!

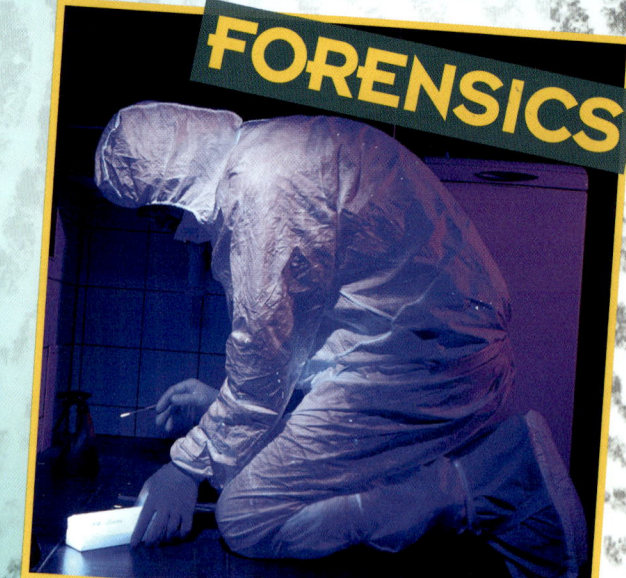

FORENSICS

A forensic scientist is a person who uses science to look at evidence during the investigation of a case. There are forensic scientists who specialize in dirt, clothing, hair, blood, and much more!

HOW TO BECOME A POLICE DETECTIVE

Before becoming a police detective, a lot has to happen. Often, detectives first go to college for 2 or 4 years to learn to write reports and analyze, or study closely and think through things. Then, they go to a special police school for 18 to 24 months. There, they train their body and mind and learn many special police skills.

Each police department has different rules for who can become detectives, but it's usually after 3 or 4 years as an officer. They may also have to pass written or other kinds of tests.

While working as a police officer, you'll learn a lot of important things that will help you when you become a police detective. You'll learn about laws and different kinds of cases.

POLICE SCHOOL

13

OTHER KINDS OF DETECTIVES

Not all detectives work for the police. Private investigators are detectives who own their own detective company. They're often former police officers. They have to pass state testing and go to a special school. Many kinds of companies have investigators to help them hire people, keep the company safe, and investigate crimes.

There are investigators who specialize in art theft, deleted computer information, missing people, fires, injuries, car accidents, boats, banks, money, and much more!

MAKE A DETECTIVE KIT!

Get a closer look at the world around you using these common detective tools: measuring tape, magnifying glass, flashlight, and **binoculars**. Use these tools to observe and take note of any **details** you see!

The government has several national organizations that do detective work, such as the Federal Bureau of Investigation (FBI) and the Central Intelligence Agency (CIA). Even the armed forces have detectives!

15

WHAT DOES IT TAKE?

A detective must be organized, or have everything in order. Each case will have a lot of details, conversations, clues, and questions! A detective also needs great observational skills to see and hear things others miss.

It's really important that a detective has great **communication** skills. They have to ask questions in a way that gets people to open up. They have to get inside people's minds for information they can't remember, don't think is important, or don't want the police to know!

SHARPEN YOUR MIND!

During a case, you'll need to remember lots of details, names, places, and more. You can start in your kitchen. Observe and take notes on everything you see. One week later, go back to your kitchen and notice what's moved, changed, gone, and new.

Depending on what part of the country they're in, many detectives learn a second language so they can speak with local people more easily.

THE TOOLS OF THE TRADE

There's a lot of awesome **technology** that can help detectives solve cases. Forensics is using scientific knowledge and methods to solve a crime. Nowadays, there's technology that can match blood, hair, and fingerprints left at a crime scene to a person or other crime. There are even tools to match a bullet to a gun!

Detectives can sometimes even use spy technology, though they have to ask a judge before they listen to other people's phone calls, record secret videos, or track people or things!

TAKE FINGERPRINTS!

Ask if you can get fingerprints for everyone in your home. One at a time, roll the top of each finger from left to right over a stamp pad. Then slowly roll the finger onto a blank index card. Label each fingerprint by which person, which hand, and which finger it's from.

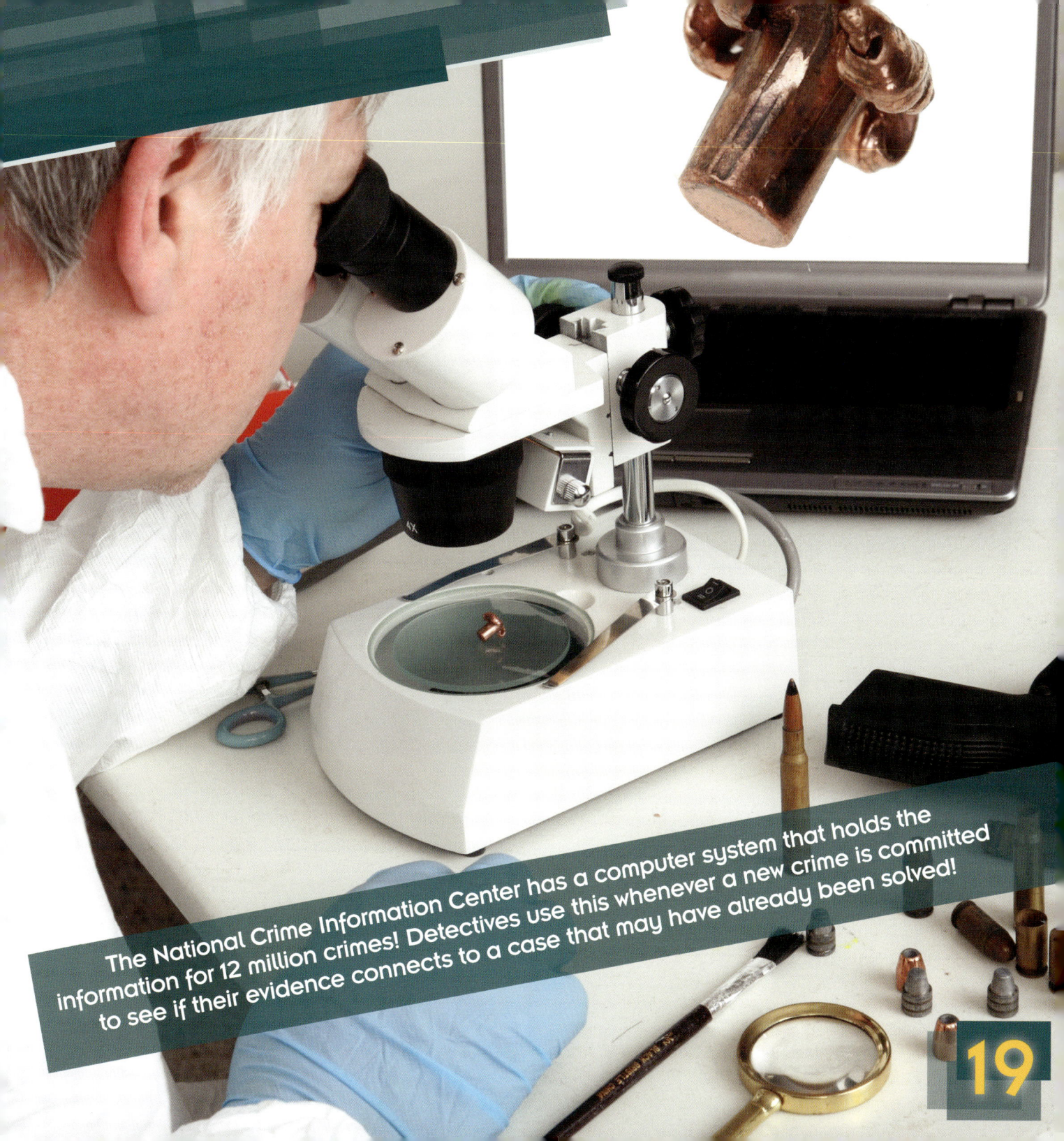

The National Crime Information Center has a computer system that holds the information for 12 million crimes! Detectives use this whenever a new crime is committed to see if their evidence connects to a case that may have already been solved!

CAN YOU HANDLE IT?

Do mysteries make your mind spin with curiosity and ideas? Do you want to solve puzzles to help other people and make your community safer? Detective work takes a lot of time. Certain crimes may even be dangerous to investigate or upsetting to look at.

If you find yourself at the end of this book wanting to know more, you'd probably make a great detective! The most important thing now is to keep your eyes and ears open. You never know what you might notice!

YOU'LL NEED

PRACTICE FINGERPRINTING!

- a clean water glass
- cornstarch or baby powder
- clear tape
- a black piece of paper
- a magnifying glass
- your finished fingerprint index cards from page 18

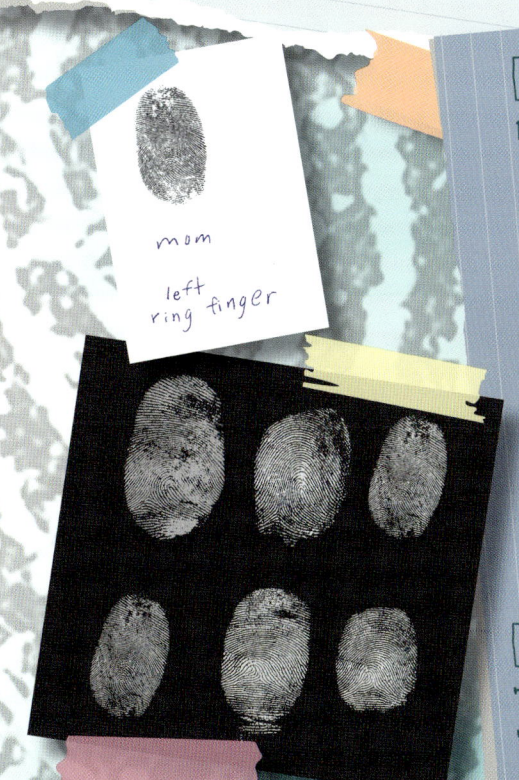

mom

left
ring finger

LEVEL 1

1. Have everyone in your home go into a room where you've set out a clean, empty water glass.
2. After you leave the room, have one person touch the glass and leave their fingerprints behind.
3. Without touching the glass, inspect it closely to find the fingerprint.
4. Sprinkle the fingerprint lightly with cornstarch.
5. Blow on the cornstarch carefully to reveal the fingerprint.
6. Place a piece of tape on the fingerprint so the powder sticks to the tape.
7. Stick the tape onto black paper.
8. Using your fingerprint index cards and your magnifying glass, compare prints to figure out who touched the glass.

LEVEL 2

Test other surfaces to see how to find fingerprints on different materials. Test a wall, door handle, metal pot, book, piece of clothing, or anything else you want!

21

GLOSSARY

binoculars: a tool that you hold up to your eyes and look through to see things that are far away

body language: movements or positions of the body that show a person's thoughts or feelings

communication: the act of sharing thoughts or feelings by sound, movement, or writing

detail: a small part

information: knowledge obtained from study or observation

investigate: to try to find out the facts about something to learn how it happened and who did it

law enforcement: groups that make sure laws and rules are followed by people and companies

puzzle: something that is hard to understand and needs thought or skill to be solved

solve: to find the answer

source: the cause or starting point of something, or a supplier of information

technology: the specialized tools, such as computers, people use to do a task

victim: someone who is harmed or suffers some loss because of a crime

FOR MORE INFORMATION

Books

Hanson, Anders. *Detective's Tools.* Minneapolis, MN: ABDO Publishing Company, 2014.

Kutschbach, Doris. *Art Detective: Spot the Difference!* London, UK: Prestel, 2013.

Van Steenwyk, Elizabeth. *How Kate Warne Saved President Lincoln: A Story About the Nation's First Woman Detective.* Chicago, IL: Albert Whitman & Company, 2016.

Websites

Detective Case Report
scholastic.com/content/dam/teachers/lesson-plans/migrated-featured-files/jandetreport.pdf
Print these detective work sheets whenever you have a case you need to solve!

Should I Become a Detective?
study.com/become_a_detective.html
Watch this video on how to become a detective.

INDEX